THIS BOOK
BELONGS TO:

_____

TWO BY TWO
The Story of
Noah's Ark

Written by Alice Joyce Davidson
Illustrated by Maggie Swanson

Regina Press
New York

God told Noah, "Build an ark.
Start making it today,
for soon I will be sending
a big, deep flood your way."

All of Noah's family worked from dawn to dark following God's orders to build a big, BIG ark.

Then they filled it up with animals —
all that they could find.
They took a male and female —
just two of every kind.

Two fierce lions, two meek lambs,
two cats and then two dogs
walked side by side to board the ark.
Next came two hopping frogs.

Two elephants stomped on the ark.
Two monkeys swung behind.
Two ponies pranced. Two donkeys danced.
Two zebras joined the line.

Two walruses came waddling on.
Two doves and blue jays flew.
The animals kept coming
and the ark became a zoo.

Then Noah and his family
loaded things to eat –
fruit and vegetables and hay
and grass and seeds and meat.

When every kind of animal
had boarded two by two,
God sent a storm that flooded the earth
just as He said He'd do.

It rained for forty days and nights,
till finally one dawn,
those aboard the ark were safe
but life on earth was gone.

When the storm was over
sunshine filled the sky.
The ark stopped on a mountain
and the land began to dry.

Noah prayed with thanks to God,
the creatures joined in too,
with chirps, and growls and loud meows
and a cockle-doodle-dooooo!

God took His brightest colors,
made a rainbow in the sky and then
God promised He would never
send big floods again.